THE **HOW AND WHY** WONDER BOOK® OF

ROBOTS

ROBIN McKIE

PRICE/STERN/SLOAN
Publishers, Inc., Los Angeles
1987

Spot-welding on a production line at a Ford car factory.

ROBOTS

Design	Cooper-West
Editor	Catherine Bradley
Researcher	Cecilia Weston-Baker
Consultant	Peter Scott
Illustrators	Hayward Art Group and Gerard Browne

Foreword

The word robot was first used by the Czech writer Karel Čapek in 1920 to describe human-looking machines designed to work for people. However, real robots working in factories in Japan, the United States and Europe seldom look like the "tin men" of science fiction.

Most scientists define a robot as a machine body that is operated by a computer, working independently of humans and capable of doing different jobs. Like other machines robots make our work easier, by moving materials, tools or other objects through programmed actions. In the future, as better computers are designed, robots will play even bigger roles in our lives.

Contents

Anatomy of a robot

Most robots look like giant "arms" and imitate the movements of the human arm and hand. All robots have to be linked to a computer that controls the robot's arm. The computer is like the robot's brain, and by changing the instructions in the computer's memory, the robot can be used for a variety of tasks. The first generation of robots was linked to very basic computers and could only do simple work like picking up and placing objects.

① Computer
Every robot is linked to a computer. Computers are used today to design and construct programs for the robots and they control all the robot's movements. A terminal is used to gain access to the computer.

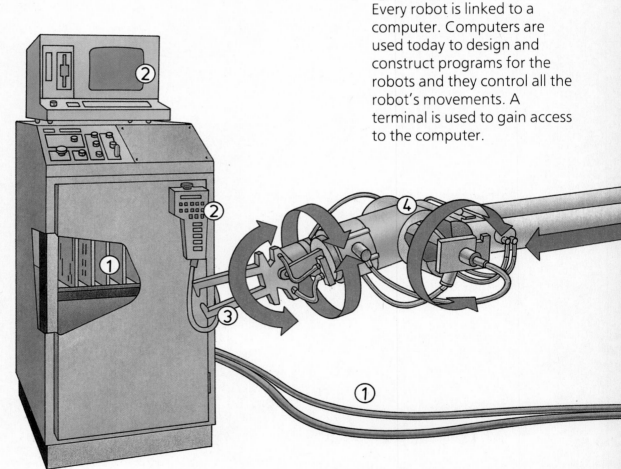

② Programming
The list of instructions fed into a computer is called a program. Robots can be reprogrammed by putting in new instructions for a different job.

③ Sensors
A robot's sensors feed information back to the computer about the position of the robot arm and about the surroundings. Generally these are force or pressure sensors.

Today, technology has developed to produce a new generation of robots equipped with "sensors." These sensors send back information about the robots' surroundings to the computer. Robots like these are capable of many types of accurate and complex work.

The industrial robot

The Unimate 2000 robot, shown here, is a typical industrial robot. Different tools can be fitted to the end of the arm — welding equipment to join pieces of metal together, for example. The computer can be programmed to make some types of robot change tools automatically. Often, "grippers" are attached to the robot's wrist and these are used for grasping objects. Some grippers work by vacuum suction. Others, used for picking up metal objects, are magnetic.

④ **Movement**
A robot is moved by actuators at each joint. These are connected by wires to the computer, which tells them what to do.

⑤ **Power**
Robot arms are powered hydraulically or electrically. The Unimate 2000 uses a hydraulic system which means it can lift heavy items. The gripper is shut pneumatically.

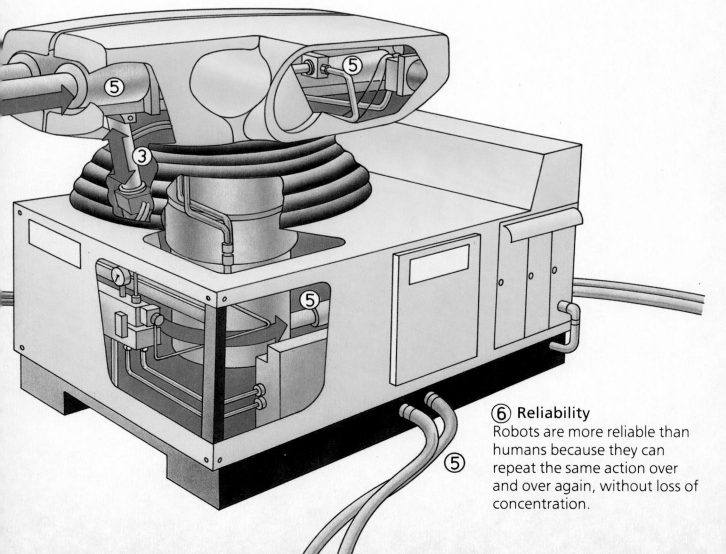

⑥ **Reliability**
Robots are more reliable than humans because they can repeat the same action over and over again, without loss of concentration.

Robot movement

Robots are designed to move in different ways. They can turn, pick up objects and put them down. To carry out these tasks, all robots need to be able to move in at least three ways: from side to side, up and down, forward and backward. This is achieved by combining several types of joints along the robot arm. A robot that can move in three directions is said to have "three degrees of freedom." Often, even the most complex robots only have six degrees of freedom compared to the human arm which has 22! The range of positions that a robot arm can reach is called its "work envelope."

▷ An unusual form of robot arm is the "Spine" robot, invented in Sweden and made up of a series of discs held together by two pairs of cables. These make the arm move while sensors tell the computer where to position the arm.

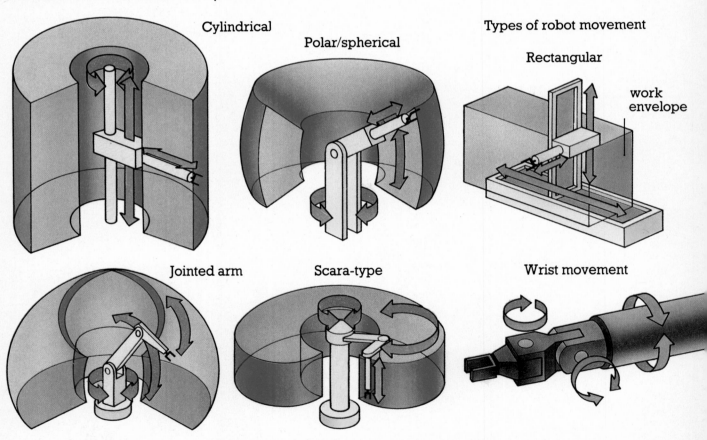

Cylindrical

Polar/spherical

Types of robot movement

Rectangular

work envelope

Jointed arm

Scara-type

Wrist movement

△ There are five types of robot arms commonly in use in industry. The cylindrical movement moves in and out, up and down, and swivels round a vertical axis. The jointed arm has a joint at the waist, shoulder and elbow. The polar (or spherical) movement is like the cylindrical movement, but uses a pivoting vertical motion. Scara-type movement is similar to the jointed arm, but has joints in the horizontal rather than the vertical plane. Finally, rectangular movement can go up and down, from side to side and in and out. The wrist movement of a robot allows for greater freedom of positioning than the arm alone.

Human control

Machines called "teleoperators" also act like robots and are used to do dangerous jobs like bomb disposal. They can be guided by their operators mechanically or by electric signals. However, they are not real robots since they need humans to guide them. They are not connected to computers and cannot act independently.

△ The Spine robot looks like a snake and has greater reach and flexibility than many other arms. It can be used for work such as spray-painting the interior of a car, where other arms may find it difficult to reach. Spine robots are yet to be widely used in factories.

▷ GADFLY is a research robot, which is completely different from other robots. It has a tool-mounting plate hanging from three pairs of rods. By changing the lengths of the rods, it is possible to give the gripper range and flexibility within a limited space. This is a "parallel" robot, which could be used for light assembly work.

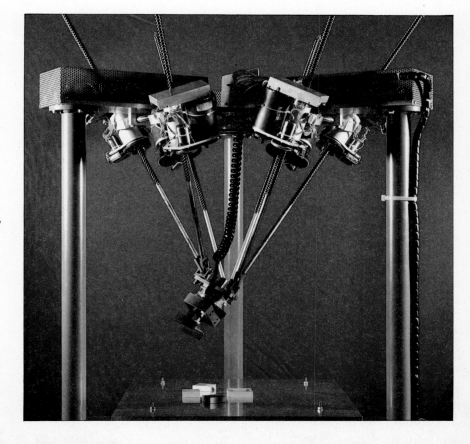

Programming a robot

A robot has to be told or taught how to operate. The set of commands that controls its actions is called a computer program. There are three ways to program a robot.

Teaching a robot

The simplest type of robot teaching is called "lead-through" programming. A human operator guides, or leads, a robot through the movements of a job. The computer memorizes the movements and the robot can then repeat the task it has been shown.

In "walk-through" programming, the operator uses a remote-control aid called a teach pendant. Controls on the pendant instruct the robot to move from point to point – left, right, up and down. Then the computer works out how to route the robot arm between these points.

▽ This method uses a skilled worker to guide the robot arm through all the stages of a job. Attached to the robot arm (1) is a special lead-through aid, or controller (2). In this illustration, a paint spray nozzle (3), is being led through the points that make up a complete work cycle. As the computer memorizes each point, the robot can repeat the action again and again.

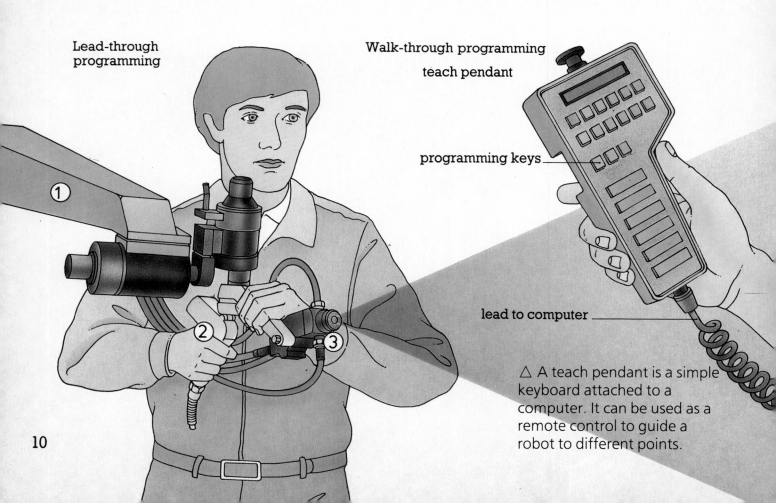

Lead-through programming

Walk-through programming teach pendant

programming keys

lead to computer

△ A teach pendant is a simple keyboard attached to a computer. It can be used as a remote control to guide a robot to different points.

▷ Using a teach pendant, an operator steers the robot through the required movements. At key points information about the robot's position is fed into the computer's memory. The robot can then repeat the set of movements. This system is used for a wide range of tasks from welding to assembly.

△ CAD (Computer-aided design) is used to plan the most efficient use of a robot system. A designer can simulate a robot's movements and watch them on a visual display unit (see inset). These simulated movements could then be automatically turned into a robot program.

Off-line programming

In the third method of teaching, an operator types exact instructions on the keyboard of a computer terminal. These instructions are then translated into a series of electric signals that guide the robot's movements. In sequence these movements build up into a complete action. Using this method, the operator can prepare new instructions while the robot is still working on another job.

Powering a robot

A robot must have strength, flexibility and a range of different programs to be useful. Electricity is the power that makes the robot work. The robot moves either hydraulically or by electric motor. Large robots that lift heavy weights tend to use a system of hydraulics.

Hydraulically powered robots

An electric motor powers a pump which forces liquid through a central cylinder connected to smaller cylinders throughout the robot's body. When the computer tells a valve to open, liquid forces a piston inside the cylinder to move. All the moving parts of the robot are connected to a system like this, and it is the backward and forward motion of the piston which results in the robot's movement.

▽ Cincinnati Milacron robots weld car bodies at Ford's Dagenham factory, UK. Each moving joint is controlled by an electric motor, which is put into action by signals from the computer. Electric motors are quiet and efficient and can do work requiring great accuracy.

Hydraulic rotary vane

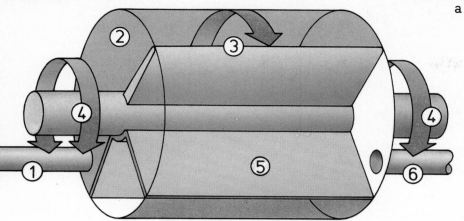

Hydraulic sections on a standard robotic unit

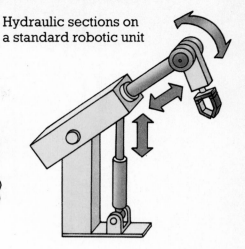

Hydraulic ram system

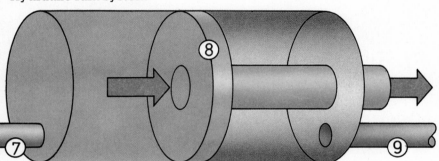

◁ The rotary vane actuator is a form of hydraulic piston. Fluid (1) is forced into the chamber (2), making the vane (3) and shaft (4) rotate until the required position is reached. It is prevented from making a complete circle by a stop (5). To go in the opposite direction, fluid (6) is forced into the other chamber. In the hydraulic ram piston system, fluid (7) is forced through making the piston (8) move forward. To reverse the action, fluid (9) is forced through on the other side.

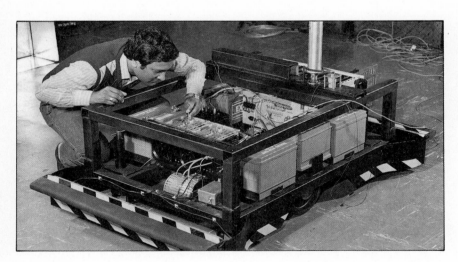

△ This prototype mobile robot from Imperial College, London, carries its own power supply. It has batteries just above the wheels.

Electrically powered robots

Usually, for making the smaller movements – reaching out, or gripping things – robot joints are powered by electric motors. The computer controls movement by switching the electric current to the robot's motor on or off. Electric robots tend to be quiet, precise, and easy to maintain, and so they are being used increasingly. There are also some mobile robots that carry their own batteries to power them.

Sensors

Humans have taken millions of years to evolve their senses. Modern technology has had only a few years to develop similar devices for robots, but already great progress has been made. Devices called "external sensors," a TV camera, for example, "feed" information in the form of electronic signals back to the robot's computer.

Electronic feedback

When the computer receives a signal it adjusts the robot's movements to match the new information received. In this way, the robot is able to react almost instantaneously to its surroundings.

▷ This Unimate robot uses four TV cameras to "see" whether car windshields are correctly positioned.

▽ This is a simple feedback control system which can be used on a robot's joint. The computer (1) sends a signal which goes through an error detector (2), and amplifier (3), to the motor (4) in the joint. This signal makes the arm (5) move. The encoder (6) senses where the arm is positioned. If the input and feedback signals do not match, then the error signal (7) will adjust the arm to correct its position.

Feedback control system

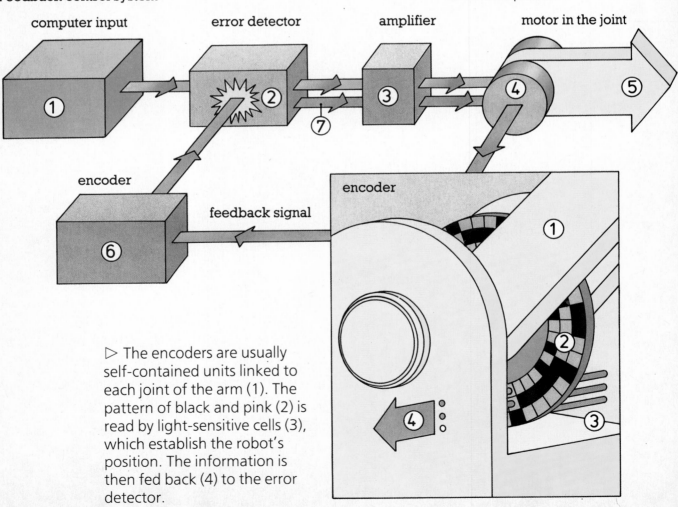

computer input   error detector   amplifier   motor in the joint

encoder

feedback signal

encoder

▷ The encoders are usually self-contained units linked to each joint of the arm (1). The pattern of black and pink (2) is read by light-sensitive cells (3), which establish the robot's position. The information is then fed back (4) to the error detector.

△ The gripper above has very sophisticated silicon touch sensors which allow it to handle fragile objects. The Omnigripper, above right, can pick up more complex shapes. It has parallel sets of fingers so that it can grasp an object. The gripper is lowered over the object and the fingers are then pushed either around the object or into it.

Touch

One important external robot sense is touch. Without it, a robot might crush fragile objects as it tried to pick them up. To prevent this, some robot "hands" are fitted with tiny sensitive pressure sensors. Once they make contact with an object, a signal is sent back from the computer, stopping the hand's movement or changing it. Thus a robot on an assembly line needs a "touch" sense to identify component parts.

Vision

Scientists have worked on robots with sight sensors for many years. One problem is teaching a computer to interpret the picture it is receiving from a TV camera.

A computer needs to have information about the height and depth of the objects it sees. The computer uses this information to build up a three-dimensional picture of an object. This is usually done by some form of illumination, such as shining a light onto the object in front of the camera. The Three-Dimensional Part Orientation System measures an object's height by calculating the exact position of a dot of light.

Pattern recognition

To make an advanced artificial vision system, like the one used by the research computer, WISARD, scientists have developed ways of breaking down an image into a pattern. A sheet of light is shone through a grid which casts a pattern of light and dark bars across a surface. Then the computer interprets the pattern using thousands of electronic devices which work simultaneously on different parts of the image by reacting to the light and dark areas.

▷ WISARD has been taught to recognize the expression on a human face. WISARD is shown an image of a smiling face which it memorizes. This image is broken down into a pattern using a grid – the lighter area at the center of the TV screen. Exactly the same pattern will never occur again, but when presented with a similar image, WISARD compares it to the memorized image. In the main picture, the blue bar graph on the TV screen shows the subject smiling. Inset, the bar graph registers that the subject is no longer smiling.

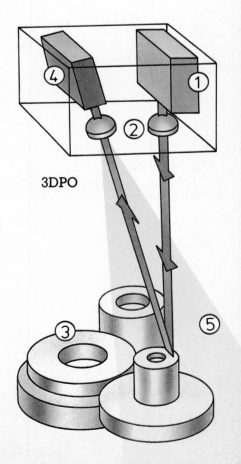

3DPO

▷ The Three-Dimensional Part Orientation System (3DPO) developed at SRI International in California has been devised so that robots can recognize specific components and sort them from others in a pile. An infrared laser (1) produces a thin beam of light which shines through a lens (2), producing a dot of light on the object (3). The sensor (4) can see the image of the dot in its field of vision (5). The computer can always measure the distance between the light source and the image of the dot. Therefore the dot also indicates the precise position of the object. A different height of object would move the dot to a different place. This movement is registered and the new height is calculated by the computer.

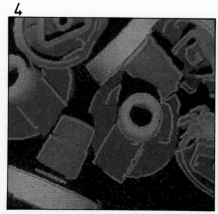

1

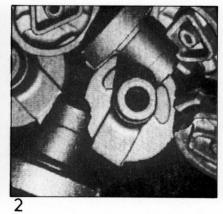

2

3

4

5

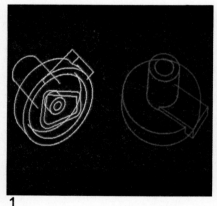

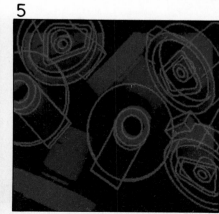

△ A three-dimensional "computer model" of the component is supplied to the 3DPO system by CAD (1). Then the ranger looks at a variety of components (2) and measures them. It picks out the highest (3) and lowest (4) points for comparison with the memorized CAD model (5).

Mobile robots

Most mobile robot-like devices today are programmed to follow trails of fluorescent material or "guide wires" buried in the ground. Such devices are already at work in offices and factories, where they carry components from one area to another. The Intelibot Shuttle at Kanazawa University, in Japan, is an example of a small robot that runs on rails. It works in the University's library bringing video tapes and books to readers and librarians.

Walking robots

The walking robots of science-fiction films are fast becoming a reality. Research projects have built robots that can walk, but these are still quite clumsy. These robots can however cover rough ground unsuitable for robots with wheels or tracks, cars, trucks and even tanks. The robot's vision and leg sensors send back signals to the computer, which then selects the best route.

▽ The Japanese designed WABOT-1 (below left) in 1973 to imitate some of the characteristics of a human. It was designed to walk on two legs. Another system of mobility for robots is following a trail of fluorescent paint. Below, we can see the robotized mail system used in the Citicorp Building in New York.

Robot to the rescue?

In Japan, the Tokyo Fire Department is currently developing a small robot crawler that uses suction pads to climb up the sides of buildings. Other robots are being designed to work under the sea, inside nuclear reactors and other dangerous places. At present, human-controlled teleoperators do this. Soon, true robots working independently under computer control, using feedback from their sensors, will replace them.

▽ This Japanese four-legged robot is designed to adapt to the ground it is covering. It uses a mixture of position and sight sensors to decide where to place its legs.

▷ The Robogate system at the Fiat factory in Italy uses unmanned trolleys to carry body shells around the factory. The trolleys follow a guide wire buried in the factory floor.

Robots at work

▽ The two cars below show the different proportions of types of workers required in the Citroën Meudon factory, which uses robots compared to a conventional factory. The traditional factory (below) needs more skilled and unskilled workers, while Citroën (below right) needs more technicians.

Today, the place where you are most likely to see a robot is in a factory. They can be used instead of people on quite complex, but rather repetitive and boring work. In car assembly plants, for example, robots weld body panels together and spray-paint car bodies. This work can cause human beings health problems – many paints contain poisonous chemicals. One day, robots may also be used to do work outside of factories. For instance, driverless tractors could be used for plowing, sowing or crop spraying.

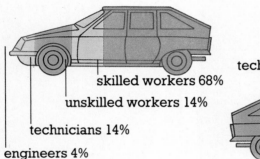

skilled workers 68%
unskilled workers 14%
technicians 14%
engineers 4%

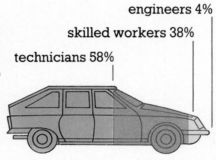

engineers 4%
skilled workers 38%
technicians 58%

▽ Most car production lines now employ robots for welding. Unimate 400 robots weld floorpans.

A robot revolution?

▽ The large Cincinnati Milacron robots take components off the conveyor belt, put them through various processes and then replace them on the conveyor belt. The much smaller IBM robot (inset) does the more detailed work of assembling a computer keyboard.

Not everyone agrees that using robots is a good idea, however. Some people worry that they could lose their jobs because robots sometimes work more quickly and efficiently and at a cheaper overall rate. Robots don't need pay and don't take vacations! Others say that robots will give people more free time for leisure or education, and that the robot industry will create new and interesting jobs.

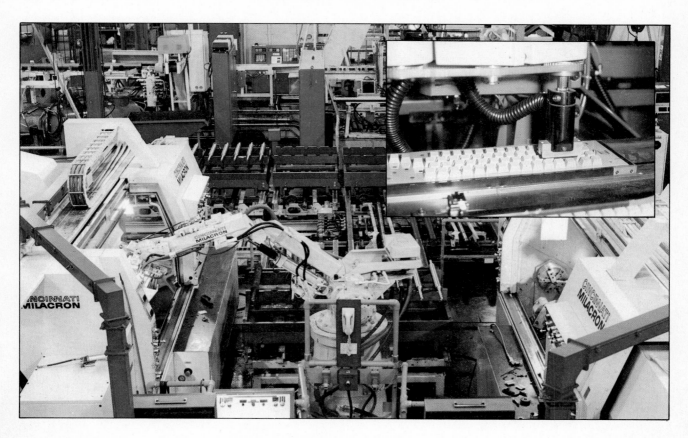

▷ This robot at the ML Aviation factory in Great Britain is drilling and deburring holes. It uses a touch sensing probe to learn the exact position of the holes to be drilled. It then calculates the correct size of drill to use, drills the hole, cleans it up and then fastens clips into selected holes.

Personal robots

Everyone dreams of having a robot that could do all the boring housework. But such a machine would have to be incredibly sophisticated. Tasks such as cleaning the house, cooking food or washing dishes seem very simple to us. Yet they involve a huge number of different movements, and no two homes are the same. Robots might require millions of instructions for any of these jobs. At present robots can only work in a stream-lined operation, such as a factory.

A few domestic robots have been built, but they are more electronic toys than real "helpers." Some can carry small objects, but they cannot perform jobs requiring intricate sensing or manipulation.

▽ RB Robot's RB5X is designed specifically for use in the home. Around the base of the robot are square-shaped collision detectors. Once in contact with an object, these collision detectors tell the robot's on-board computer to change instructions and steer the robot clear of the obstacle.

◁ This fun robot built in California is fitted with a versatile gripper and is capable of carrying out many different tasks – including watering the flowers!

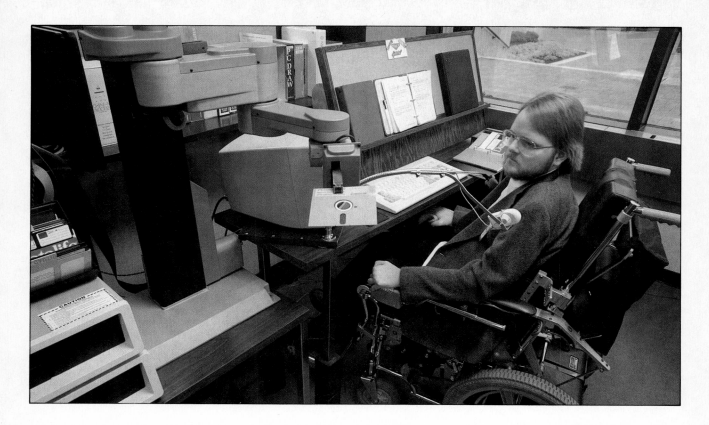

△ The RTX robot built by Universal Machine Intelligence can be used in industry, in the laboratory and to help the disabled. It is being used in the United States to set up a workplace for people in wheelchairs. In this picture the RTX is bringing a floppy disc to the computer.

A helping hand

Nevertheless, robots are beginning to do some work to help people. In the research laboratory, the Meldog Mark IV is a robot "guide dog" that has a map stored in its computer brain and is fitted with ultrasonic sensors. With these it can detect obstacles and guide people past them.

Wheelchairs fitted with small robot arms can also help disabled people with such tasks as eating or turning the pages of a book.

△ Meldog has been developed by the Japanese to help blind people. It has TV and other sensors to recognize the area ahead. Its computer compares the information from the sensors with the map stored in its memory and then sends a signal to the human owner. This machine has yet to prove itself more useful than a dog.

23

Educational robots

Robots are becoming increasingly popular as aids in education. Linked to personal computers, they can help to teach programming, geometry, design, and many other subjects in an exciting way. There are two main types of educational robot: floor robots and those with robot arms.

Turtles, buggies and other robots

Floor robots are linked to personal computers by cables or infrared beams that can carry complex signals. With these links, the robot's movements can be controlled by programming the computer. Often floor robots are fitted with pen holders. Because the computer has been carefully programmed, floor robots such as the BBC Buggy and the Turtle can be made to draw complex and elegant shapes. To control the Turtle's movements a computer language called LOGO is used.

▽ The BBC Buggy is an easy-to-make floor robot. The cover (1) protects the control board (2), which converts instructions from the computer into signals for the driving motor (3). The chain (4) transmits power to the wheels (5), and allows for accurate control. The pen holder (6) carries a pen which can be lowered. The Buggy has two sensors: a light sensor (7) and an infrared sensor (8) which can follow pre-marked lines drawn on the floor. Bumpers (9) tell the computer if the Buggy has hit an object.

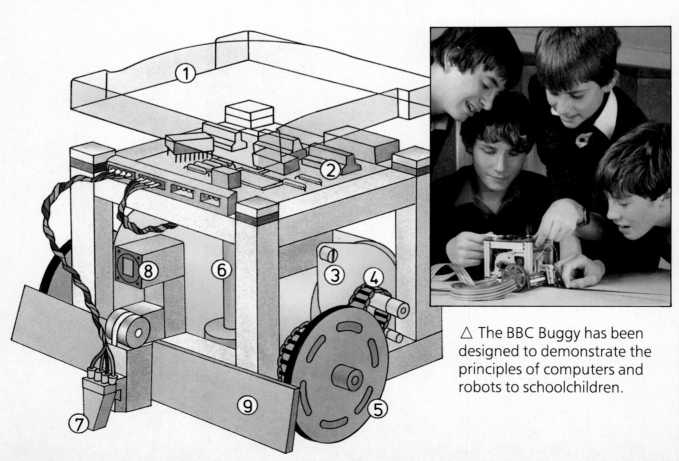

△ The BBC Buggy has been designed to demonstrate the principles of computers and robots to schoolchildren.

Learning made easy

LOGO is simple enough for beginners to understand and in the process of drawing up a program both adults and children can learn a great deal about computers and mathematics.

Simple, inexpensive robot arms are also available. Linked to personal computers, they can be programmed to lift and move objects. Like floor robots, working with robot arms can be extremely helpful in learning about programming.

▽ The Feedback Armadillo turtle (left) has two independently driven wheels. It can be instructed to chart its course on paper by lowering a pen. The Valiant Turtle (right) uses an infrared link to its computer, in place of a cable.

▷ The Armdroid is unusual in having a three-fingered gripper. It is a small robotic arm and is useful for demonstrating arm movements in teaching.

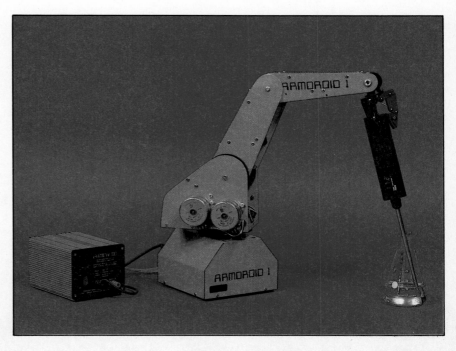

Intelligent robots

As we have seen, robots have been built to behave in sophisticated ways, for example, to respond to spoken commands. But even the most advanced robot cannot match human behavior in complexity. Robots are only as clever as the computer program that controls them.

Computers can hold enormous amounts of information and can do thousands of complex calculations in less than a second, but they cannot react to anything that is not contained in their program. At present, most computers make decisions by running through long lists of possible solutions to a problem until they reach one that is correct. However, a great deal of research is taking place to develop completely new supercomputers that will use what is called artificial intelligence, or "AI" for short.

▷ Developing their work on a humanoid robot, the Japanese have now designed a research robot WABOT-2. Its computer brain can read sheet music and it can play requests on an organ. The PANA robot (far right) is drawing a portrait from life. Its computer is taking information from vision sensors and converting this into lines which the robot is drawing.

▽ Tomy has been taught to recognize the human voice. It can be trained to respond to eight spoken commands.

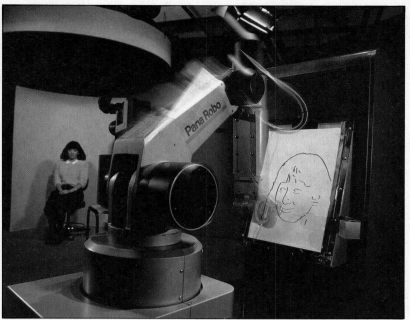

△ Recognizing voice and language patterns is one of the areas in which artificial intelligence is making strides. This voice-activated computer is being developed so that in the future computers could be linked directly to robots, which would be programmed by the human voice.

What is artificial intelligence?

Recent advances in computers that use artificial intelligence do not solve problems in a step-by-step way. AI computers should be able to compare things and use information learned in one area to help solve problems in another. In this way, a computer could develop a way of thinking similar to human common sense. If the research is successful, a true AI computer would think in the same way that a human being does, but very much quicker.

The future

The science of robots – robotics – has only developed over the last 30 years but already great advances have been made. The future of new generations of robots depends on the rapid development of intelligent computers.

A robot world

Many experts think that by the year 2000, most large-scale factories will be run almost entirely by robots, with just a small staff of human overseers. Robots linked to a central computer system will maintain the flow of components from warehouses to the assembly line where other robots will assemble the finished product.

There may even be rail networks using unmanned computer-controlled trains to take the products to be sold. Simple personal robots may help people with their shopping or serve food in restaurants.

▽ This is one of the latest high-speed supercomputers, the Cray 1-S/2000. It can compute one billion operations in a second. Such advances will increase the capabilities of robots in the future.

A new space age?

Space is a hostile environment for humans, which makes it a good place to use robots. Already unmanned landers, Viking 1 and 2, have been used to explore Mars. The United States plans to build a manned space station by the end of the century and robots will be used to perform routine tasks and maintenance. Robot space vehicles could explore the planets, or even be sent on missions to the nearest star.

▽ Already some robots are used as helpers in fast-food restaurants. Their abilities are limited, and they serve mainly to attract customers.

▷ This Orbital Maneuvering Vehicle is being developed to operate from NASA's Space Shuttle. It will deliver or retrieve satellites which the Shuttle cannot reach itself. This is one of several space robots being worked on at the moment.

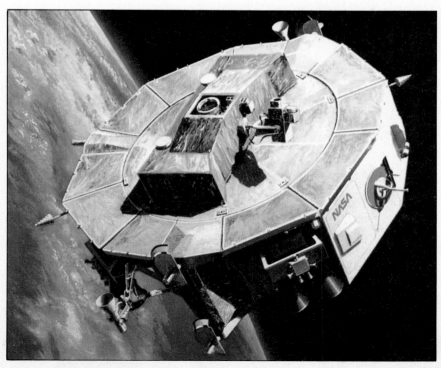

Datechart

1920

The Czech playwright Karel Čapek invents the term robot in his play *Rossum's Universal Robots*. The word robot is derived from "robota," the Czech word for forced labor. In the play, the robots rebel and take over the world.

1942

Writer Isaac Asimov outlines three laws of robotics which dictate how robots should behave if they were to become intelligent and not be a threat to humans.

1947

The Hungarian scientist von Neumann lays down the basic principles for the design of computers. With the advent of computers that could do rapid calculations, it became possible to integrate the many different processes involved in operating a robot.

1948

The British build, at Manchester University, the first computer which actually stores its program of instructions.

1956

George Devol, an American inventor, develops the idea of robots for use in factories.

1961

The first industrial robot is used in the United States in a General Motors car factory in Trenton, New Jersey. Unimation Inc. is set up by George Devol and Joseph Engelberger to produce industrial robots. The company is still in business today and is owned by Westinghouse.

1968

Shakey, the world's first sophisticated mobile robot, is built at the Stanford Research Institute. It has a television camera, touch detectors and a radio link to a computer.

1976

One of the most sophisticated space probes ever built, Viking 1, lands on the surface of Mars. It carries a teleoperator arm, two computers, chemical and photographic laboratories, and a weather station.

1985

Japan has installed over 64,600 robots in its factories. The figure compares with 13,000 such robots in America, 20,500 in Europe and 2,623 in Britain.

Glossary

Android A robot that looks like a human being.

Artificial Intelligence An attempt to use computers to imitate human reasoning.

Computer A flexible machine that uses small electronic circuits to make rapid calculations, to process information and to control operations. Computers can process thousands of instructions per second.

Degrees of Freedom The number of movable joints that a robot arm possesses.

Feedback The technique by which a robot alters its movements according to information received from its sensors.

Gripper An attachment to a robot arm used to pick up small objects.

Hydraulics The use of a liquid to transmit force by, for example, driving a piston inside a cylinder.

LOGO A simple computer language widely used to control the movements of educational robots such as the Turtle.

Robot A computer-controlled machine that can be programmed to do different types of work independently of humans.

Robotics The study of robots.

Sensors Devices like TV cameras, microphones, touch pads, and others that provide a robot's computer with information about its surroundings.

Index

Acknowledgements
The publishers would like to thank the following individuals and organizations who have helped in the preparation of this book:
Alan Moutrey of the Robotics Association, Dr Igor Aleksander of Imperial College, Austin Rover, Babcock FATA, Cincinnati Milacron,Colne Robotics, Economatics, Fanuc Robotics, Foster-Berry Associates, GE Calma, Professor I. Kato of the University of Waseda, Japan, Mitsubishi Heavy Industries, Stanford Research Institute, Spine Robotics, Taylor Hitec, Tomy UK, Toshiba, Unimation, Universal Machine Intelligence, Wagner Indumat and thanks to Dorchester Typesetting.

Photographic Credits:
Cover: Hank Morgan/Colorific; *title page*: Foster-Berry Assoc. for Tomy UK; *contents page*: Cincinnati Milacron; page 9, Spine, Marconi Research; page 10, J. Mason/Science Photo Library (SPL); page 11, Fanuc, GE Calma; page 12, Cincinnati Milacron; page 13, Imperial College; page 15, Austin Rover, Hank Morgan/SPL, Imperial College; page 16, Stanford Research Institute; page 18, Professor Kato, Dan McCoy/Colorific; page 19, Mitsubishi; page 20, J. Mason/SPL; page 21, Cincinnati Milacron, IBM, Taylor Hitec; page 22, Mark Wexler/Colorific; page 23, Universal Machine Intelligence, Mark Wexler/Colorific; page 25, Art Directors, Colne Robotics; page 26, Foster-Berry Assoc. for Tomy UK; page 28, Hank Morgan/SPL; page 29, Mark Wexler/Colorific, Boeing.

PRINTED IN BELGIUM BY
proost
INTERNATIONAL BOOK PRODUCTION